Gilead Books Publishing
Corner Farm
West Knapton
Malton
North Yorkshire YO17 8JB UK
www.GileadBooksPublishing.com

First published in Great Britain, January 2013
2 4 6 8 10 9 7 5 3 1

British Library Cataloguing-in-Publication Data:
A catalogue record for this book is available from the British
Library.

ISBN-13: 978-0-9568560-8-1

The publisher makes every effort to ensure that the papers used
in our books are made from trees that have been legally sourced
from well-managed and credibly certified forests by using a
printer awarded FSC & PEFC chain of custody certification.

Cover design: Nathan Ward
Cover image: Vivek Chugh
Illustrations: Anna Tash

Contents

Foreword

Preface

Acknowledgments

Foreword

The Bible continues to be a source of inspiration and challenge to the many people who read it on a daily basis. It is also a valuable treasury full of stories that have been told and retold down through the generations in different formats and locations to a variety of audiences who may be less familiar with its content.

This is still true for the 21st century. Kay Brown, the author of Come, See This Man, has produced ideas and material that can be used in a variety of settings, not least in the context of Sunday Worship.

As an experienced Lay Reader in the Church of Scotland, Kay has chosen familiar incidents from the gospels and retold them using language that introduces new insights into these familiar stories.

A number of these meditations could quite easily be used to replace a sermon, allowing the reader to take time to draw the listener into the rhythm and power of the prose, which tells the story with integrity and empathy. Equally the material may well be used to retell a familiar gospel story to help illustrate a sermon, or be used in a more informal setting as part of an epilogue.

I'm happy to commend this material to a wider audience knowing that whatever way it is used, it will be a blessing to all who take time to engage with its themes and short Bible reflections.

Rt Rev Albert Bogle BD MTh, Moderator of the General Assembly, Church of Scotland

Preface

Then leaving her water jar, the woman went back to the town and said to the people, "Come see a man who told me everything I ever did. Could this be the Christ?" They came out of the town and made their way towards him. John 4: 28-30

A few years ago, as part of a series of evening services during Holy Week, I was invited to give an address, but not a sermon, based on Jesus' entry into Jerusalem. After much prayer and thinking about how to do this, the result was Chapter 3, 'Who is This?' On being asked the following year for the same approach from two other churches, 'Anointed' and 'Come, See This Man' came into being.

People who had been at the services told how they felt moved, changed and encouraged in their faith during the meditations, and suggested that they should be made available in print. My first response to this idea was a very firm, 'No!' However, several meditations, much encouragement and lots of prayer later, this book was born.

Writing in this way is a whole new experience for me. I have only been able to do so with the help and inspiration of the Holy Spirit. I am continually surprised, excited, fearful and amazed at how God prompts, encourages, equips and inspires us to go wherever he calls us.

The beginning of my own journey goes right back to Sunday School times, when I began to 'look' for God everywhere—in those days, especially in the sky! As the years passed, I continued to seek God and to search deeper, which led to an amazingly exciting and challenging period of change for my husband and I. We became involved in a prayer counselling ministry, which enabled us to allow Jesus to begin a healing process in us that will continue for as long as we live.

We were invited to come and see a man who knows all about us. And, like the woman at the well, we discovered that even though he knows everything about us, he still loves and accepts us and entrusts us with his Good News. Our lives were completely changed and we were led into full time ministry.

These meditations are the result of Bible reading, much prayer, reflection and learning to listen to God combined with the experience and tremendous privilege of praying with others for healing of body, mind and spirit.

The words of the woman at the well inviting all her neighbours to, 'Come and see a man who knows all about me,' echo down the years inviting us today to meet with Him afresh. May you be blessed as you read and may you be drawn closer to 'This Man' who loves us beyond our understanding.

Many Blessings,

Kay Brown
Falkirk, January 2013

Acknowledgments

My heartfelt thanks to all who have encouraged and prayed for me during the writing of these meditations. Special thanks have to go to Marion Balish and Patricia Martin who have patiently read each completed chapter adding their prayers and encouragement along the way.

Thank you to the Right Rev Albert Bogle, Rev Melville Crosthwaite, Rev Peter Neilson, Marion Balish, Anne McKean and Patricia Martin for so generously contributing their commendations, all of which were humbling to read.

Chris Hayes of Gilead Publishing without whose encouragement and sound advice this book would not have been possible.

Last, but certainly not least a big thank you to my husband John for all his support, help and patience with me as I struggled with the computer!

To John

Come, See This Man

Then leaving her water jar, the woman went back to the town and said to the people, "Come, see a man who told me everything I ever did. Could this be the Christ?" They came out of the town and made their way towards him. John 4: 28-30

'Come, see a man who told me everything I ever did.' This ringing, confident command from a woman, who is an outcast in the village. Her behaviour is appalling. She flouts all the normal rules of living, so none of us have anything to do with her, and yet here she is urging us all to come and see a man.

Whoever he is, he must have had some effect on her, because she's shouting that he knows all about her, surely she hasn't been speaking to this man on her own. Dreadful!

Yet, 'Come, see a man.' The words cause something deep within to be stirred, touched as if an arid part of the soul has been moistened, softened. Something profound, eternal, has touched your being.

'Come, see a man.' Imagine him, whoever he is, speaking to this woman—her of all people! Confusion and resentment jostle for a place in your thinking. You struggle with your feelings. Then she says he has promised to give her living water that will mean never thirsting again. Well! Your confusion knows no bounds.

Despite this confusion, and resentment, something deep within your being begins to long, indeed thirst, for this living water. And so you are drawn to join all your neighbours as they leave the village to go to Jacob's well.

'Come, see a man.' The feeling of confusion is now tinged with anticipation and excitement as you hurry towards the well. Nothing like this has ever happened before. After all, in this part of the world, life is fairly hum drum, not a lot changes.

What on earth are we all thinking about, following this woman so eagerly? We must be crazy, especially in the heat of the day, when we would normally be indoors resting.

'Come, see a man.' The words feel like an invitation to meet with someone special, but common sense tells you that this whole thing is ridiculous. After all, no self-respecting man would talk to a woman who is on her own. So how could he offer her water that will mean she will never thirst again, whatever that might mean? He can't really be anyone special, can he?

Your mind swirls with a mixture of confusion, hope, excitement and, of all things, anticipation—even a little fear. You ask yourself, 'Who can this man be?'

'Come, see a man.' Here you are, at the well, and all you can see is a group of dusty, grubby looking men, all of whom look a bit disreputable. What a letdown. What on earth is all the fuss about? No sign of water here, only heat and dust. We would have to draw water from the well to get a drink.

Then it happens, the group parts, and you find yourself face to face with the man at the centre of it all. As he looks at you, and you look at him, the inexplicable happens. You are filled with a sense of being washed clean, as if water is pouring all over you. At once your mind is filled with the words from Isaiah:

Here is my servant whom I uphold, my chosen one in whom I delight; I will put my spirit in him and he will bring justice to the nations. Isaiah 42:1

13

This feeling of water being poured over becomes an invading, liberating sensation of being brought to life, filled with the water of life. All your fears and apprehensions are washed away in the flow. In this man's presence, all desires are relegated. He is the water of life. His presence has touched your very soul! You will never thirst again.

'Come, see a man.' She was so right. He does know all about us, and in the knowing, even loves us. Secure in that love, she came to share his love with us. She came and witnessed because she had been forgiven—released from all that had been wrong in her life. This woman, who had gone to the well at midday, thirsty, alone, rejected—returned, full of His living water, coming to share his love with us, who had rejected her.

'Come, see a man.' Only Almighty God could have the power to have complete knowledge of us all. The silence is tangible, the awe is all pervading, as we stand there in the presence of the most amazing man we have ever had the privilege of meeting, and he is, of all people, a Jew.

This living water is none other than the presence of Almighty God in our lives. And even we Samaritans have to bow to this man Jesus, to acknowledge that he is bringing salvation to our lives. He is who he says he is, the Messiah, whom the prophets foretold.

Come and see this man today and he will fill you with living water, so that you will never thirst.

Come, see this man and he will cleanse you from your sins.

Come, see this man and he will wash away your fears.

Come and see this man and he will restore your very souls.

Come, see this man, who went to the cross for each one of us and rose from the dead so that we can drink the water that wells up to eternal life.

Come, see Jesus Christ King of kings and Lord of lords.

Father, help us to worship you in spirit and in truth. Fill us with your Holy Spirit, so that in the filling, we will be released into your truth.

Pour over and into us the water of life, until we cry in unison with the woman at the well, 'Come and see this man, who knows all about me and in the knowing still loves me.'

Amen.

Anointed

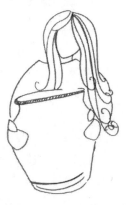

Jesus turned towards the woman and said to Simon,
"Do you see this woman? I came into your house. You
did not give me any water for my feet, but she wet my
feet with her tears and wiped them with her hair. You
did not give me a kiss, but from the time I entered has
not stopped kissing my feet. You did not put oil on my
head, but she has poured perfume on my feet.
Therefore, I tell you, her many sins have been forgiven –
for she loved much. But he who has been forgiven little
loves little."
Then Jesus said to her, "Your sins are forgiven."
The other guests began to say among themselves, "Who
is this who even forgives sins?"
Jesus said to the woman, "Your faith has saved you; go in
peace." Luke 7: 44b – 50

'Do you see this woman?' Jesus' words scared me to the depths of my being. I really did not want anyone to look at me, never mind to actually see me, to actually be seen! That was what was so scary, even threatening. I felt naked as I stood there in their midst, in the presence of all these important people.

My mind yelled at me that I should never have come here. My heart seemed to freeze within me. And, my very physical being felt as if it had been dried up under their accusing stares.

'Do you see this woman?' How dare *he* point the finger at me? I brought all that I had to *his* feet. I even used my hair to wash *his* feet—my very hair. No self-respecting woman would ever unwind her hair in public, and she certainly would never wipe another's feet with it.

As fear, anxiety, even terror all pushed and pulled and tore at my very soul. And, as I stood there my hands and my hair dripping with the oil of the precious perfume, how I wished that I had stayed at home.

There I was sinning again, unwinding my hair in public and wiping a man's feet with it into the bargain, living up to my reputation as a sinner. My behaviour towards Jesus was outrageous, and really unthinkable. No wonder Simon the Pharisee was looking at me with such contempt.

Yet, the power of His words—'Do you see this woman?'—seemed to be reaching down into the depths of my being, piercing the darkness and weariness of my soul with a gentle light and warmth.

I still daren't look any of them in the eye, the feeling of condemnation was too strong. It was as if I was rooted to that spot with all my pain, misery, and sin. How could I look all those good, respectable people in the face?

'Do you see this woman?'—Suddenly I begin to really hear what Jesus was saying to Simon. He's telling him a story about two men, each of whom owes money to a money lender. One owes far more than the other and yet the money lender cancelled both their debts.

Simon began to look really worried at this point. He became even more agitated, when Jesus asked him which of the two men would love the lender more. 'I suppose the one who has the biggest debt cancelled,' replied Simon.

It was at this point that I started to feel the light and warmth begin to glow deep within me, a feeling of gratitude permeated my gut, and then began spreading upwards in my being, touching the edges of my heart. The feeling of warmth and light increased with every word that Jesus uttered and I found my head beginning to lift.

'Do you see this woman?' The sound of Jesus' voice and his words were touching my pain and misery. I had never experienced anything like it before. A well of hope began to bubble gently in the depths of my being. I began to allow myself to dare to believe that the rumours about Jesus bringing healing and forgiveness might just be true, even for me.

Everyone in the room was riveted to the spot, not a sound could be heard as Jesus told Simon exactly what he, Simon, had been thinking about. Then I knew that Jesus did know all, all about each one of us in that room. Joy bubbled up within me, almost taking my breath away as that knowledge claimed me. *He* knows *me!*

'Simon, do you see this woman? I came into your house. You did not give me any water for my feet, but she wet my feet with her tears and wiped them with her hair.' I could feel myself being lifted. As if raised from death and my heart was warmed.

My head lifted up a little higher.

'You did not give me a kiss, but this woman has not stopped kissing my feet.' My mind stopped yelling and *his* peace stilled me, stilled my mind with what I recognised as His love, a love beyond my understanding.

My head came up a little further.

'You did not put oil on my head, but she has poured perfume on my feet, therefore I tell you her many sins are forgiven; for she has loved much.' My body was flooded with *his* oil of healing, my head anointed with oil, and my cup overflowed.

'Your sins are forgiven, your faith has saved you go in peace.' I was now free to look him full in the face. A face, holding all eternity in his gaze, looked back at me, and I knew that he knew all that I had ever been, and all that I ever would be. And in the knowing, he loved me with a love that would follow me all the rest of my life and that I would dwell in *his* house forever.

I am so glad that I didn't stay at home!

Lord, help us to have the courage not to stay at home.
Draw us to where you would have us be.
Lift our heads from avoiding your gaze.
You, who have gone to the cross for us,
And have assuredly risen again.
Call us into eternal life with you.
And as we look at you,
pour into us your vision for resurrection living.
Amen.

Who is This?

When they brought the colt to Jesus and threw their cloaks over it, he sat on it. Many people spread their cloaks on the road, while others spread branches they had cut in the fields. Those who went ahead and those who followed shouted, "Hosanna!"
"Blessed is he who comes in the name of the Lord!"
"Blessed is the coming kingdom of our father David!"
"Hosanna in the highest!" Mark 11:7-10

Jerusalem! At last. My heart's desire is realised.

To be here in Jerusalem for the Passover is way beyond my expectations. My sons said I was too old at eighty to make the journey. But they were wrong. I had to come I had to be here this year Oh, not only because it could be my last opportunity. I know, in my heart of hearts, that to be in Jerusalem this year is more important than anything I've ever done in my life.

I've been a good Israelite all my life. I have tried to keep the commandments, although, that's been difficult at times, and I've honoured the Law and the Prophets. Despite all this I have an inner sense that I'm searching for something more, something so important that it could change my thinking, even my understanding—a quest? And I know that God is the source of all these feelings.

Standing here thinking like this is holding me back. I'm going to be left behind in the crowd, and then my sons will be saying that I'm certainly too old to be here.

The excitement of the crowd rushes into me, gripping me, filling me with awe as we push and jostle our way towards the Temple. Excitement? No! This entire experience is more, much more, than simply excitement. I feel deep inside my being as if I'm being drawn towards meeting with God himself. That's impossible. The God of our Fathers doesn't meet with ordinary people like me, especially in the middle of a noisy, jostling crowd, even if we are on our way to the Temple. It's an experience like no other I've ever known.

I hear the words of the great psalm of my forefathers resounding from person to person through the crowd,

'Let Israel say: His love endures forever!'

I hear my voice, 'Yes! Yes! His love endures forever.'

The whole crowd unites in praise, 'Let the house of Aaron say: His love endures forever.' a cry that echoes down the years

Yes! Yes! This is all part of the faith of our fathers.

A cry again from the crowd, 'Let those who fear the Lord say, His love endures forever.'

Yes! Yes, God is to be feared. But there's more.

What can that *more* be? I've achieved the desire of my heart. I'm here, in Jerusalem, so what more do I need?

The sense of reaching for more is filling my heart. No, it's deeper than that. I feel as if my very soul is being called from down the years, away back before I was born, called to the most important meeting of my life. I can't explain it, but my whole future depends on this meeting. Huh! My age must be affecting my thinking; I must be losing my reason.

The shouts of the crowd are becoming louder, 'Hosanna to the son of David! Blessed is he who comes in the name of the Lord.'

'Hosanna to the son of David!' My heart beats faster as this shout reverberates through the crowd.

My heart is stirred by a strange yet powerful excitement. My excitement grows.

'Blessed is he who comes in the name of the Lord.' The name of the Lord, I feel an urge to push against this crowd, all swaying together, a mass of moving bodies that I can't seem to get through. This feeling of 'calling,' grips my soul with an intensity so strong that I push with all my strength against the crowd. I have *got* to see what all this excitement is about.

The realisation that there is a person at the centre of all the excitement hits me with a fear that leaves me shaken to the roots of my being. My legs turn to water. The struggle to remain on my feet is almost too much for me. I've never experienced anything like this, ever. Eagerness overcomes my fear, so I push hard against the mass of people. Fear still grips me, grips me in the throat, as if threatening to choke me into submission, but, submission to what? I *have* to see who this person is in the middle of the crowd. Who *is* he at the centre of all this uproar?

This shouting 'Hosanna!' is almost like worship. But, 'You shall have no other God's before me.' Surely this is blasphemy? I push forward, desperate to see and at the same time, afraid of what I will see. 'Hosanna! Hosanna!' the sound of the praise rings in my heart lifting my spirit with a renewed sense of hope.

'Blessed is he who comes in the name of the Lord!' The crowd parts, and there before me is the reason for all this adulation—a man on a donkey! He's surrounded by a group of dusty, dirty, poor looking men. Fear and shock tear at my gut. This just can't be. Now, they're throwing palm branches down in front of him. This surely *is* blasphemy. I have honoured the God of our Fathers, the God of Abraham, Isaac and Jacob all my life and now they are treating this man on a donkey as if he is God himself.

I am rooted to the spot. My being weeps with disappointment and rage. Fatigue drains the strength from every part of my body. Worse still, my life seems to be spread before me as if in one long hopeless journey. Why was I so desperate to come to Jerusalem? I could have stayed at home and worshipped God in the safety and security of my own Synagogue and kept my peace of being. Instead, all the excitement and anticipation of my desire to visit Jerusalem destroyed, destroyed by a man on a donkey.

'Hosanna! Hosanna!' Then a strange inner silence. Silence is filling my being, as if from before I was born. The 'call' to meet with Almighty God seems to be rushing along the road of my entire life to meet me, filling me with a vision of love so strong that I can scarcely breathe.

He turns his head, this man on a donkey, and his eyes meet mine. My life's journey is complete; he is the 'call!' He is the reason I'm in Jerusalem. He *is* the something more.

'Hosanna! Blessed is he who comes in the name of the Lord.' This man on a donkey—the God of Abraham, Isaac and Jacob—he, who knows every step of the life he has given me, calls me to be his, forever.

Lord, when your call touches our lives, release us from the fear of responding to you.

Lord, you often meet us in the unexpected; release us from our stubborn resistance.

Lord, when the confusion of life threatens to swamp us, help us to reach out for your hand.

Lord, when we begin to recognise who you truly are, open our hearts to receive you.

Amen

Simon of Cyrene

As they led him away, they seized Simon from Cyrene, who was on his way in from the country, and put the cross on him and made him carry it behind Jesus."
Luke 23: 26

The surge of the crowd is almost suffocating as it forges its way towards Golgotha. I can feel, even taste, the fear that's mixed with the anger and resentment at the sight of this fearful spectacle.

The cruelty of it makes me sick, sick to the pit of my stomach. I really feel like running away. I only wish I'd stayed at home, Passover or not. At least I would have been spared the horrors of a crucifixion. No, not one, but three.

I need to get right out of this crowd, now. Yet, my entire being seems to be in a battle that's holding me here despite myself. The crowd is imprisoning me, its power, and its movement, linked with a strange longing in me to see this man Jesus for myself.

His reputation is amazing, miracles, healings, teaching that's changed lives, his compassion for the poor. All around me people are speaking about his goodness. So why? Oh why is he being crucified?

I feel as if I'm being held prisoner to my own feelings of fear, frustration and anger at this injustice before me. I can't bear being here, but I just can't tear myself away. It's as if I'm really meant to be here.

Suddenly, I'm at the front of the crowd and the three figures with their crosses are staggering straight towards me. I can't cope with the horror of this. The soldiers are cracking their whips at the three men, prodding and kicking them as if they were animals. It's too much. How can they carry these heavy crosses and suffer being beaten at the same time?

As if from beyond my soul's awareness, I *see* the third prisoner, the man Jesus. He is so ordinary. He's filthy dirty, streaked with blood, staggering all over the road under the weight of that huge cross. Ugh!

You would think that after all his healing miracles he'd be able to save himself. Even with all his wise teaching, he's never uttered a word in his own defence. Crazy, crazy behaviour, maybe he really is mad. Oh! Who knows? I wish I was anywhere but here, anywhere at all.

Yet the entire crowd seems to be gripped by something so powerful and strong, that we are held together and compelled – yes, compelled to walk with Jesus.

Jesus is falling forward, the cross pinning him down, holding him captive to its weight. The crowd surges and moans as if in concert with Jesus' struggle.

I feel myself being hauled forward, the vice-like grip of the soldier piercing my skin like a thorn ramming into my flesh.

We come face to face, this Jesus and me, and my eyes are drawn to his crown of thorns. It's piercing his forehead with a ferocity that makes me shudder, shudder to the depths of my being. I can't stand this. These Romans are barbarians.

Then, his cross becomes my cross, as the soldiers heave it into place on my shoulders. How am I ever going to carry this cross? It's crushing me down, crushing me, and they're expecting *me* to carry this burden all the rest of the way to Calvary.

The bile rises in my throat; I'm choking, choking with rage and fear. Why choose *me*? And all for a man of doubtful background. Huh!

His eyes meet mine, and my very soul is seared with certainty. He's not mad. He knows me. He knows my heart. He even understands my disdain of him.

Oh! The honour of bearing this cross.

Suddenly the cross has no weight at all. My entire being is flooding with a depth of love, a feeling so new to me as to be almost frightening in its power. This love is taking me beyond myself, allowing me to reach out and embrace his love, in the lifting and carrying of the cross.

My heart is pierced with the knowledge that I'm now part of something eternal—yes, eternal. I, Simon of Cyrene, am now a part of His sacrifice for the world and His sacrifice for me, even for me.

The honour is mine; the blessing is mine, to carry His cross, even a little part of the way.

Lord, when we find ourselves in places we don't want to be, touch us with your grace.

Lord, when we struggle with the tasks of life, touch us with your comfort.

Lord, when we feel unloved, touch us with your love.

Lord, your gift on the cross is beyond price.

When the weight of our cross is too heavy to bear, lift it from our shoulders, so that we may walk afresh with you. Amen

The Centurion

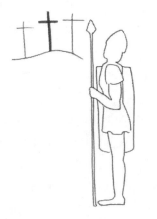

It was now about the sixth hour, and darkness came
over the whole land until the ninth hour, for the sun
stopped shining. And the curtain of the temple was torn
in two. Jesus called out with a loud voice, "Father into
your hands I commit my spirit."
When he had said this he breathed his last.
The centurion, seeing what had happened, praised God
and said, "Surely this man was the Son of God."
Luke 23: 44-47

I've been to the depths of despair and all because of a
Jew on a cross. I'm forced to live in this God-forsaken
part of the Empire, or I certainly wouldn't be here. No-
one in their right mind would choose to live in this

desert of a place, and as for the people. Well, words fail me.

Here am I, a Roman soldier, a Centurion no less, and this mere Jew has turned everything I've ever believed and understood upside down, and all in one day.

I'm a Roman. We're rulers of the world, and yet, this Jew, hanging here, dying on a cross, seems to have more authority than anyone I've ever met. No! Not possible. The Emperor is my only authority. He has to be, or my life wouldn't be worth living. After all, the Emperor has to be bowed down to, and obeyed as if he were a god. If anyone does know about authority, I should. Being a Centurion, my men have to respond instantly to my commands.

This man's authority is profoundly different. It's more powerful than any authority I've ever come across, and yet, somehow, there seems to be a love there too, I must be mad.

As he hangs there, the wound in his side gaping wide, we soldiers cast lots for his clothes, as if he is no better than the scavenging dogs, which roam around looking for every scrap of rubbish they can find. I feel as If I am losing my very soul to a darkness that seems to be creeping out from my heart and engulfing every facet of my being with hopelessness.

We just carry on throwing the dice for this man's clothes, well, there is really only his robe, and that's a poor rough piece of material.

As he hangs there in agony, hands torn open, bones crushed and exposed by the nails, bleeding, O how they are bleeding. Hands that are supposed to have been used to heal all sorts of illnesses, even lepers. Huh! That's too much for me to even contemplate. These Jews have some crazy ideas and no mistake.

His feet, hammered into place on the cross and held there by huge nails. Feet which have walked all over this God-forsaken land, so that this Jesus could supposedly tell anyone who'd listen about the love of God. The love of God? No God of love would surely ever show his love by allowing one of his supporters to die in this appalling way.

I don't like this at all. This is no ordinary crucifixion. I've never felt like this ever, and I've been in charge of numerous others. This *is* different. I feel as if I'm in some kind of battle. My very teeth clenched hard together as my being tries to resist this creeping darkness, like a hell.

Yet, even as hopelessness and despair seem to devour me, I meet his eyes. From deep within him shines a love so strong that I'm almost dazzled by its piercing power. But, this darkness seems to be fighting for me, for who I am. Yet, at the same time Jesus' power seems to be fighting for me too.

I'm just not thinking straight, I don't like this crucifixion at all. It is like no other I've ever known.

Who is this man?

No! No! I feel fear like I've never felt it before, not even in the thick of battle. My entire being feels as if it is being scourged, and as for this pain in my heart, well that feels like nails being pushed into the very core of my being. I just want to vomit it all out and get rid of this unbearable war raging inside me. I need somebody to help me. Ridiculous! A Centurion needing help.

Oh! Who is this man Jesus, that he can cause me to experience such pain and fear?

Still we cast lots for his garments.

'Father, forgive them for they do not know what they are doing.' Forgive them? Forgive us? What next, how can some non-existent god forgive? We Romans are the true rulers. But, of course, this Jesus thinks he's the King of the Jews. Rubbish! Just like this place of human rubbish, Golgotha.

I feel his gaze burning into me, no condemnation, only acceptance, no fear, only courage, no hate only love. And I hold up the vinegar soaked sponge to his lips, when it happens. The darkness of the battle within me seems to be sucked up into the darkness spreading across the sky. No light! No sun! Only a terrible feeling of tearing inside me as I hear his voice calling, 'Father, into your hands I commit my spirit.'

Father! Father! What kind of a god does this man have that he can call him Father? 'Into your hands,' how can he say, 'Into your hands?' when his god allows him to be crucified? Nailing him to a cross, 'I commit my spirit.' What kind of god can this be, that this Jesus is still willing to give this god his spirit? Indeed, *commit* his spirit to him, after suffering such complete degradation.

Even as my mind swirls in the storm of fear and confusion and the darkness deepens, a light of truth begins to penetrate this maelstrom of experience. Can this man really be the Son of God?

'This man truly is the Son of God!' The words seem to be wrenched from me, as if despite myself. Peace engulfs my soul. Hope bursts forth in my heart. Joy rushes upwards from my very bowels.

Love, his love, shakes me asunder with its power, and as the storm rages and roars around us, I know that this cross is a symbol of God's love. Love for *me*, a mere Roman, as if forgiving me my role in this hideous death.

The storm of doubt and fear has been replaced with his love and joy. Peace envelops me, as if like a gift of grace, touching me with forgiveness. He truly is the Son of God. And I a Roman bow to God's Son, this man on a cross, this Jesus. He has won. The victory is His.

Lord, when we find ourselves in a storm of fear and doubt, touch us with your gift of peace.

Lord, when we find ourselves doubting even ourselves, fill us with your gift of faith.

Lord, when we find ourselves searching for your forgiveness, anoint us with your presence.

Amen

He is Risen!

"Woman" he said, "why are you crying? Who is it you are looking for?" Thinking he was the gardener, she said, "Sir, if you have carried him away, tell me where you have put him, and I will get him."
Jesus said to her, "Mary".
She turned towards him and cried out in Aramaic, "Rabboni!" (which means Teacher) John 20:15-16

Lord! Lord! Where are you Lord? What an end to such promise. Jesus dead and buried in the tomb. An end to hope, an end to joy, an end to love and forgiveness, just a dead end to all he promised. My whole life is dead. How can I live without him? The pain of losing him is like being dead, and at the same time, having to go on living. Why? Oh, why, did I believe that Jesus was the Messiah?

No one ever treated me the way he did. He restored my self-respect. He lifted me from a life of emptiness bringing healing and restoration to my soul. As for his teaching, well, that was amazing. His teaching about God as our Father was so vivid that I wanted to know God more. He opened up a whole new understanding of the scriptures for our entire group; and even more importantly for all the crowds of people who flocked to him, and now, nothing.

Lord, Lord where are you? Even your tomb is empty. There's nothing of you left, nothing at all. Not even the stone they used to seal your tomb is in place. It's gone as well.

The empty tomb, such a beautiful day, birds singing, life all around me touching my eyes as if inviting me to see, to feel, to enjoy, yet nothing is reaching my heart. Jesus promised to be with us forever, but he's not here, only a black empty tomb, a big black empty hole, just like my heart right now. He even had the power to heal me from my demons. I'll never forget his power rushing into me bringing such a release and freedom that I danced for joy.

No joy now, only misery in my soul, because they have taken away my Lord and I don't know where he is. What *will* I do? What will we all do without him? He was our master, our friend, our teacher, our Saviour. We even thought that he was the Messiah. And now all that remains of our hopes and dreams is an empty tomb.

The garden is so beautiful, birds singing, the morning air so fresh. But, *they have taken away my Lord!* Distress catches my breath, the tears stream unchecked down my face in a river of despair; I want to shout at the birds to be quiet. Have they no respect for my grief? Still they sing, the birds, and still I weep for my Lord, whom they have taken away.

Then, through the tears I *hear* your voice, as if right here beside me, reaching out to me from beyond the grave, promising that you will be with us forever. But you're not, are you? You're crucified, dead and buried, and your body isn't even in the tomb. How's that for promising to be with us forever? I'm choking with the disappointment of your broken promises.

Still the birds sing and still I weep, I just don't understand all this pain and confusion. It feels so very cold. The cool fresh breeze of the early morning catches my face, drying patches of tears as if in compassion and gentleness. Yes, that's it, gentleness and compassion, so like you Lord. If only you were here, and *still* the birds sing.

But now they seem to be saying, 'Peace to you' 'Hope to you', 'Joy to you' Not possible! I'm allowing my grief to cloud my thinking. This is amazing. For somehow my heart feels calm, as if the gentleness of the air is flowing deep into my being. This gentleness feels like a warmth, even love, reaching out to me and touching my soul, reaching into the bit that death cannot touch. As if saying to me that there is no death. Impossible!

A suffocating blanket of misery continues to wrap itself round me. Yet this breeze, this gentleness, is reaching through the blanket, as if seeking to comfort me in my grief. Lord! Lord! If only you had saved yourself, I wouldn't be feeling like this. I can't believe he's not here, one more look, then I must go back to the other Disciples.

Two angels! This is like being struck by lightning. My fingers grip the wall of the tomb as my eyes struggle to accept what they are seeing, my legs give way, my whole being is filled with fear and hope, in a confusion that threatens to completely overwhelm me.

'Woman, why are you crying?' The angel's voice cuts me to the core. 'Woman, why are you crying?' Why am I crying? Don't they understand my grief? They're sitting right where Jesus' body should have been, and they ask me, 'Why are you crying?'

'They have taken my Lord away, and I don't know where they have put him.' As I utter these words, my voice sounds so empty and far away, bereft, bereft of all Jesus enabled me to be. Why, oh why, is he not here? Even these two angels don't seem to understand my loss. Not even a body to visit. What's the point of visiting an empty tomb? My grip on the wall of the tomb loosens, and I turn empty away.

Still the birds sing, and still, I weep, I weep for my Lord whom they have taken away. Strangely, as I turn away, this breeze of gentleness seems to be supporting me, filling my being with love, Lord where are you?

The morning sun is dazzling. It seems brighter than usual. And, as I turn from the tomb, I'm dazzled by its brilliance. My soul feels torn in two, as I walk from the blackness of the tomb into the brilliance of the sun. So strange. The brilliance is blending with the breeze, filling my emptiness.

I'm suddenly aware of the gardener, he's here early, I suppose the cool of the morning is good for working, before it becomes too hot. He's bound to know where they have taken Jesus, I'll ask him.

'Woman, why are you crying? Who is it you are looking for?' His voice penetrates my mind with a strangely familiar ring. The sound of his voice and the gentle breeze become one and the same. This is impossible! I'm tired, fearful, too confused, to be able to think clearly.

'Sir, if you have carried him away, tell me where you have put him and I will get him.' This breeze, it's taking my breath away. I can't breathe! Jesus used to take my breath away with his teaching, if only he were here now, I'd give anything. Everything! To have him here beside me now.

'Mary' It can't be! It's not possible! Jesus is dead! But, that voice! He spoke like no other could. I cannot bear to look. It can't be him. Even as I hesitate, his power envelopes me in his love. I dare to turn towards him, 'Rabboni!' erupts from my lips. My soul explodes with joy as I see him there in the dazzling light of the sun.

He is risen! He is alive! This dazzling brilliance, which bathes us both, is no ordinary brightness. It's emanating from Jesus. He *is* the brilliance... the bright morning star.

As I reach out to touch him, he tells me, 'Do not hold on to me for I have not yet ascended to the Father. Go instead to my brothers and tell them, I am ascending to my Father and your Father, to my God and your God.' Understanding floods my soul, Jesus has conquered death itself. He is Risen!

I want to fall on my face before him, but he's gone. As my heart calms and my being stills I become aware of the breeze, no, His breath, empowering me, as if for eternity itself. He has been with me in all my grief and pain, all my doubts and fears.

My companion through my bereavement was no mere morning breeze, but the wind of His Spirit. His presence with me all the time, His presence, filling me with Himself, enfolding me in His love, enabling me to keep seeking him, even in an empty tomb.

All the weakness has gone! My whole being feels washed through by the power of His love, filled with His risen power. My heart is held in His love. My mind is full of His light and His amazing truth. Jesus is Risen from the dead! I dance for sheer joy. I join the birds in singing His praises. He is Risen! He is alive! Jesus is alive!

Lord, when doubts and fears assail us, touch our souls with faith and courage.

In the darkness of grief, shine your light of hope into our hearts.

When life's problems threaten to overwhelm us, fill us with the breath of your Holy Spirit.

May we know your risen power in our lives, by the presence of your Holy Spirit, around us and in us.

Lead us ever forward in resurrection living with you. Amen.

No Stranger

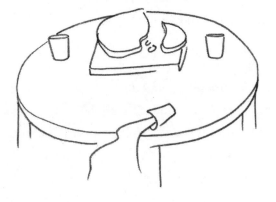

When he was at the table with them, he took bread,
gave thanks, broke it and began to give it to them. Then
their eyes were opened and they recognised him, and he
disappeared from their sight. They asked each other,
"Were not our hearts burning within us while he talked
with us on the road and opened the Scriptures to us?"
Luke 24: 30-32

Our doubts and disappointments are banging around
in our heads like hammers, destroying the tiny kernel
of hope that Jesus could be alive. Not possible! He's
crucified! Dead and buried! And, dead *is* dead *is* dead!

After all we saw it all happen; Cleopas and I
experienced the horror of it, as we huddled together
for comfort. There was no comfort, only life-sapping

fear, in case we were recognised. The evil, the cruelty of the nails. Our terror at the blackened sky, a sky that seemed to portray the menacing wrath of God as Jesus died.

So, the women can't possibly be right about seeing angels and him being alive. How can he be? Yet, our women are convinced he's alive, and some of the men declare that what they are claiming is true. Still, this hammer of disappointment, indeed devastation, bangs on and on inside our thinking as we walk and talk together on the road to Emmaus.

This road to Emmaus, it seems to be the hardest journey we've ever taken. The very stones underfoot feel as if they are the rubble of our lives, now that Jesus is gone. This journey is like walking in a grey fog of loveless emptiness, a place devoid of hope. Our feet are throbbing as if in accord with our thinking, and our hearts are filled with a sense of betrayal.

Devastation is overwhelming us, almost as if it has the power to destroy even that kernel of hope that keeps trying to break through. Neither of us understands how all this evil and misery has come to pass. Jesus, who was going to save Israel—now dead and buried. All our hopes dashed to pieces, like fragments of grit on the road.

Oh! How our souls ache. Our abject misery brings us to a halt. And, as we stand there united in our despondency, he comes and joins us, this fellow traveller, a complete stranger—and yet, is he? He appears as if from nowhere, suddenly here by our sides, and now he's asking us, 'What are you discussing together as you walk along?'

What are we discussing? Has this man not heard what has been happening in Jerusalem? Surely he knows about Jesus and the rumours that he is alive. How can he not know?

Anger threatens to overcome us and we want to shout at him. But, we don't. Instead, we begin to tell him of our hurts and our fears, even our devastation at having all our hopes dashed, when Jesus was crucified. He was going to be our Messiah! Now he's dead! Or is he? Our women claim he is alive!

Confusion, doubt, hope and misery seem to have become one big stone blocking our journey to Emmaus, sapping our strength of purpose.

His next statement shakes us to the core. 'How foolish you are, and how slow of heart to believe all that the prophets have spoken!'

How dare he, a stranger, tell us that our faith isn't good enough! Stranger? There's something familiar? No! We've never seen this man in our lives. Yet the emotion of his words is having a strangely powerful effect on us. It's as if the stone of confusion, doubt and misery is slowly being rolled away.

He certainly knows the Scriptures. Our hearts are almost exploding with excitement as he explains Moses and the prophets to us. As if opening up in our very souls, an understanding and a vision we've never had before. Or have we? There's something familiar in all this. No! No, there's not! Who does he think he is anyway, accosting us on the road and telling us that we are 'foolish and slow of heart.' Slow of heart, indeed! Can he not see that our hearts are heavy, weighed down with the loss of our master and friend, not to mention all the crushed hopes for Israel!

Oh! This journey. Well, everything has changed since Jesus died. Nothing can ever be the same again—ever. We're both agreed about that. It's as if making the journey has heightened our fears and confusion about Jesus. Talking and discussing the rumours that Jesus is alive has only made the pain in our souls worse. That is, until this stranger joined us. The power of his words is like a balm to the soul. He's so ordinary, this man, this stranger, who has drawn alongside us on the road. Yet, somehow he's extraordinary—strange!

Now we're even more confused than before as we hear ourselves say, 'Stay with us, for it is nearly evening; the day is almost over.' What on earth are we doing inviting a complete stranger to stay with us, especially one who has insulted our level of faith in one breath and soothed our souls in the next. He agrees, this stranger, to stay with us. There is something so compelling about him, even familiar. No, he *is* a stranger, we can't allow our feelings of misery to confuse us like this.

He breaks the bread, this stranger. He shares the bread, this stranger. He disappears from our sight this stranger. But, he's *not* a stranger! It *is* Him! Our bewilderment knows no bounds as we stare at each other in amazed delight.

He's not a stranger! He's not a stranger! He's alive! He's alive! He's alive! Jesus is alive! Our hearts are still burning within us, and our whole being feels as if we are set on fire. A fire so fierce as to reach our very souls, and yet the flame of this fire is so gentle, wrapping us in a security and warmth—his risen presence with us. This stranger, who is no stranger at all.

Jesus fills us with his love, a love beyond our imagining, bringing new life, new hope, and new vision into our hearts, our souls and our lives. We have to go back to Jerusalem and tell the others that we have seen the Lord.

We have seen the Lord in his risen power, and now, we know that Jesus walked the road to Emmaus alongside us. You see, he's been there, every step of the way. He knows all about our fears and doubts, all about our agony of soul, all about the terrible confusion that assailed us. This stranger, who is no stranger at all, loves us enough to walk with us through the valley of our despair, sharing with us our agony of doubt. But he does not leave us there. He walks the road of life with us forevermore—this stranger, who is Jesus. He, who rolls away the stones of our living, in a glorious explosion of resurrection love, bringing us from death to life. Jesus is alive!

Lord, when our doubts seek to overwhelm us, draw alongside and take our hand in yours.

Lord, when confusion seems to rob us of faith, draw alongside and breathe new faith into our hearts.

Lord, when the road of life threatens to overwhelm us, draw alongside and hold us up.

Lord, when we only see you as a stranger, roll away the stones of living, so that you are revealed.

Amen.

No Doubter

Then he said to Thomas, "Put your finger here; see my hands. Reach out your hand and put it into my side. Stop doubting and believe."
Thomas said to him, "My Lord and my God!"
John 20: 27-28

Well, the other ten say they have seen him. But, I can't even begin to think that what they are saying might be true. It's just not possible. I've thought and thought about their claim, but, it's too big a 'but', to cope with. I will only be able to believe this if I can actually feel the nail marks with my own hands. Then I would know.

Anyway the pain and disappointment of losing him is too, too much. I can't even allow myself to contemplate the possibility that their claims might be true. What if Jesus really is alive? No, the idea is beyond imagining. It's mind blowing, terrifying, demanding and challenging all rolled into one and I cannot cope with it.

After all I saw him die!—admittedly from a distance. I saw him being taken down from the cross, wrapped in the grave clothes and laid in the tomb of Joseph of Arimathea. I even saw the stone rolled into place. And, no one has ever come back from the dead before—have they? It would only raise my hopes beyond anything I've ever known, if I allow myself to listen to them. After all, their claim defies human reason.

I was so sure Jesus was someone special. I'll never be able to forget him. He taught us truths about life as God's people. He had a way of stirring the minds—No! It was the very souls—of his listeners, and that included us, his closest friends.

We often discussed, even argued. And, of course, James and John pushed and jostled in an effort to gain special favour with Jesus. But, despite these very human problems, Jesus raised us above our petty rivalries and doubts and opened up a vision of the power and love of Almighty God for us. Take the healings he performed, even the miracles, I had no doubts, when I witnessed his power and authority over sickness and even death, that he was the Messiah, the one sent by God.

When he healed the daughter of Jairus, we were all touched to the core of our being with the mere idea, never mind the reality, of that little girl being raised from the dead. I knew then, just because I knew. And nothing would have convinced me otherwise—that this was God's true kingdom in action.

But! Now? The doubts and fears fight for space in my being and I feel as if I'm in some kind of battle, good against evil, caught between doubt and knowing.

Oh! God! Why did you allow all this to happen to me? You gave me a vision of yourself in the very person of Jesus. You allowed me to begin to understand your word as never before, your compassion, your love and your care. And all embodied in Jesus, whom I thought was the saviour of Israel.

But now, I only feel emptiness and betrayal. Yes Lord, I feel betrayed by you. I feel as if you have abandoned me, robbed me of my dearest friend. Mind you, you did the same thing to Martha and Mary when Lazarus died. You robbed them of their brother.

Then, Jesus raised Lazarus—from death in the tomb into life overflowing with joy and freedom and deliverance. Life restored! The life of a brother restored to his sisters. What a mind-blowing, terrifyingly-wonderful happening. It was then that I would have given my all, everything I had, for him.

I even wanted to go to Jerusalem and die with him. I suppose, if I'm honest, I knew then that he would have to die. And, although the knowledge registered at that point, was that there had to be more, much, much more! Now I can't fathom what!

But, then the other disciples claimed that not only had he appeared to them, Mary had been first to actually see him and speak with him. A woman! Women are not reliable; they're far too excitable and prone to exaggerate. Yet, Jesus taught us to respect and work alongside women. Certainly, Mary has changed. She has matured during our time together, becoming rather lovely and, although I'm reluctant to admit it, quite a wise person.

This whole thing is more frightening than ever, because, if he is risen, the implications are beyond my understanding. Jesus crucified, dead, buried and now resurrected! Excitement, hope and fear, all roaring around in my brain, like a runaway camel train kicking up the dust and dirt of doubt and confusion. Surely it's not wrong to doubt? Especially about something as momentous as this might be! If it is true that he has risen, then, I am commanded; indeed I am committed, to lay down the rest of my life for him. Yet, how can he possibly be alive? No mere human could possibly conquer death.

But then, I can still see him feeding the five thousand; cleansing the lepers; giving that poor man born blind his sight; and of course right within our own group, Simon Peter's mother-in-law being healed. Oh! If only my mind would stop churning with all these thoughts and feelings of confusion, and as for calming the storm, that was truly awe-inspiring!

Reason tells me that no ordinary person could possibly accomplish such acts of amazing power but, he's dead and buried and now I just need to get on with my life.

What if? Just, what if the other disciples are right, and they really have seen Jesus alive!!

Oh the power of that thought, the very idea of it is sapping my strength. And, my heart feels as if it's filling my chest, I can hardly breathe. The idea that he may be alive is gripping my soul. It's overwhelming, exhilaratingly life-giving!

I need to speak to the others again. I need to know. I need to understand. I need to put all this right with them. They are all my friends. And, we have worked together, prayed together and walked the roads together with Jesus. Jesus, whom we all called, 'Lord', and trusted not to let us down.

He did tell us not to be troubled or afraid and he did promise his peace. So, maybe he is alive, just as they all claim. That's strange. All the confusion and all the anguish of the 'camel train' has settled, and I've got to admit—even for a thinking man—that my being feels strangely expectant, as if waiting.

Right now that expectancy has been overturned and in its place is blinding certainty. He's here in our very midst and I know he has come especially for me. Saying by his presence that he loves me enough to appear again in this upper room, so that I might believe.

As we stand there facing each other, I'm overwhelmed by the glory of his risen presence. And as he invites me, 'Stop doubting and believe,' I almost fall over in my eagerness to touch him, and yet, and yet, I don't need to. His wounds, visible to us all, are the marks of his sacrifice for all mankind.

I feel my soul sing and shout throughout my being as my voice utters, 'My Lord and my God.'

Lord, when we find ourselves doubting, touch us with your gift of faith.
Lord, when we struggle to understand, touch us with your love.